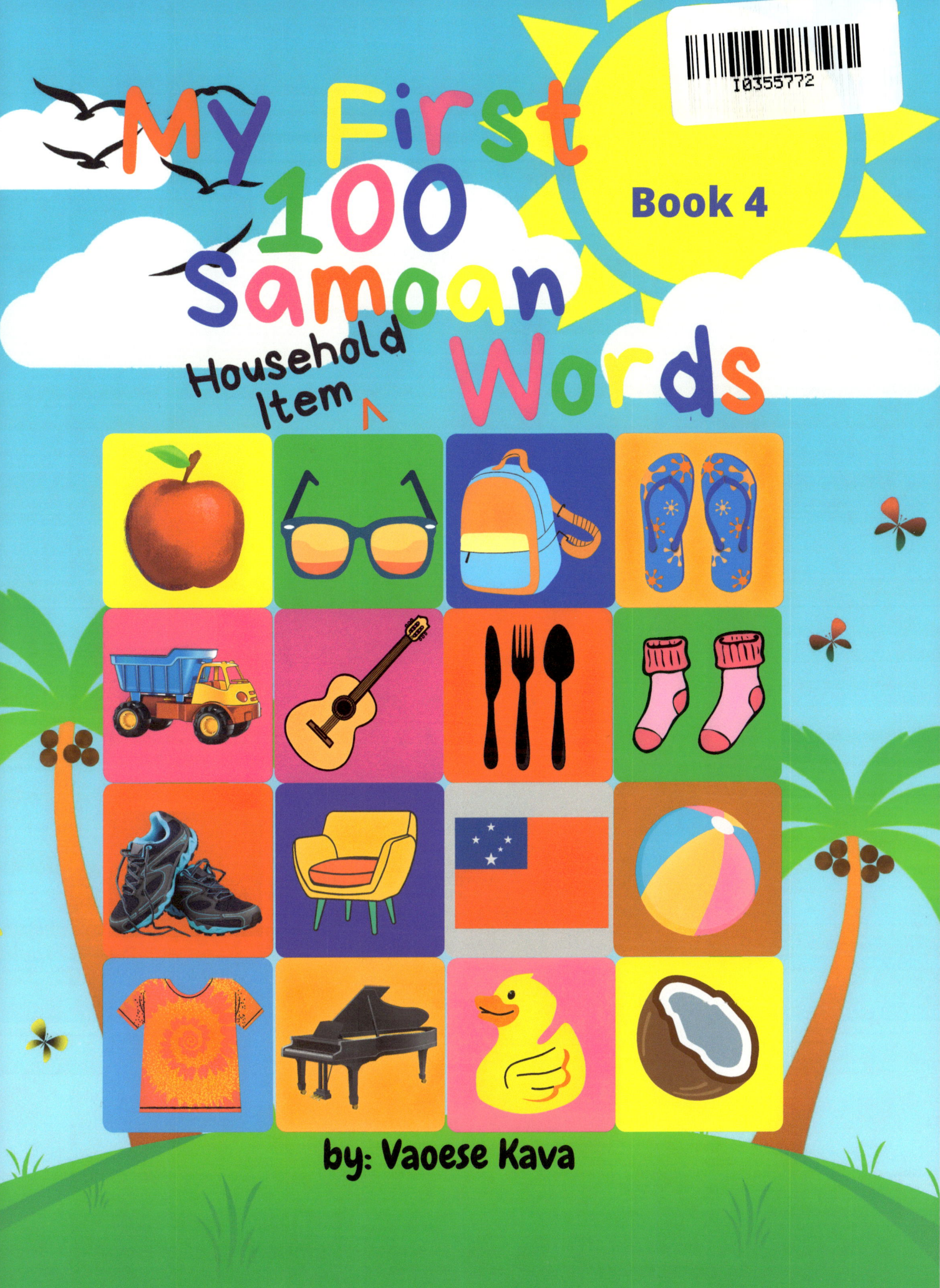

Dedicated to my dear Aunty
Ta'alolo Frontina Noa Aiono
Love you always and forever

My First 100 Samoan Household Item Words - Book 4
(presenting popular Household item names in Samoan & English)
Copyright © 2022 by: Princess Mariana Publishing
All rights reserved. No part of this book may be reproduced
in any manner whatsoever without written permission of the
author and publisher. Except in the case of brief quotations
and reviews. Thank you for your support and for
buying an authorised edition. For more information, pls.
Contact: #VaoeseLimutauKava :
on Facebook & Instagram
Written By: Vaoese Kava
ISBN 978-0-6451622-9-5   (hardcover)
ISBN 978-0-6455496-0-7   (paperback)
ISBN 978-0-6451622-1-4   (eBook)
Distributed Worldwide
First Edition July 2022

PRINCESS
MARIANA
PUBLISHING

apu / apple

meata'alo / toy

polo / ball

Pepe / Baby

tapu ta'ele / bath tub

fa'afanua / globe

moli 'aina — orange

paipa ta'ele — shower

meaalofa — present

fa'apa'u falaoa — toaster

keke — cake

matauila — light bulb

tipolo — lemon

Aiga — Family

ta'avale pepe — stroller

salu — broom

molī — lamp

pinati — peanuts

sitolōperi / strawberry

se'evae ta'alo / sport shoes

fuāmoa / eggs

pepe meata'alo / doll

pato meata'alo / rubber duck

tagapepa / paper bag

fa'i pula / banana

la'au / tree

ofu vae / pants

ofu tino / shirt

masini ta mea / washing machine

pepa faleuila / toilet paper

kapisi — cabbage

totini — socks

teine — girl

letiō — radio

fa'amalu — umbrella

ogaumu vave — microwave

aniani — onion

Tinā matua/Tamā matua — Grandma / Grandpa

palasi selu ulu — hair brush

api — notebook

laula'au — leaf

fagu susu — baby bottle

fua kiui

kiwi fruit

ofu mafanafana

jacket

teutusi

envelope

ili

fan

'au faitoto'a

door knob

fale 'ie

tent

kukama — cucumber

susu — milk

uila — bicycle

falaoa — bread

'ie 'afu — blanket

pulou — hat

avoka

avocado

taupega

swing

apa inu

soda

pusa 'aisa

refrigerator

aluga

pillow

ato fa'afafa

backpack

popo — coconut

tama — boy

lapisi — rubbish bin

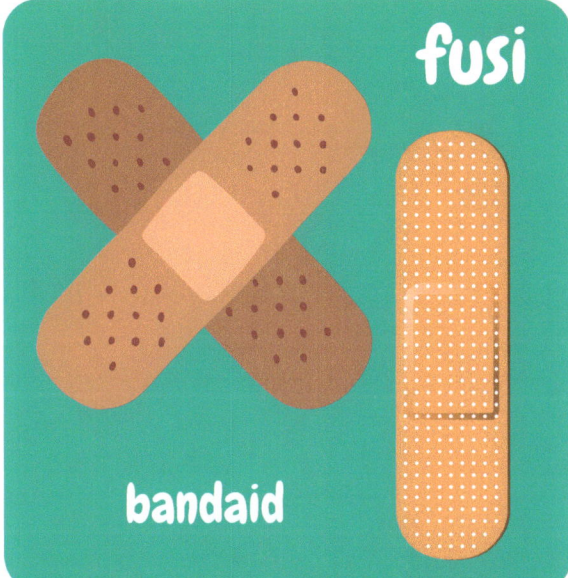

fusi — bandaid

moa vao — lawnmower

sipuni la'au — wooden spoon

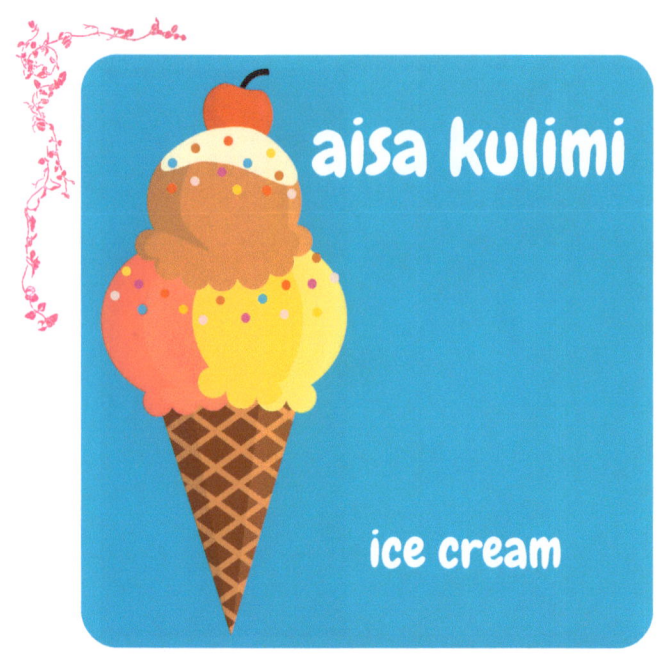

maukeni — pumpkin

logo — bell

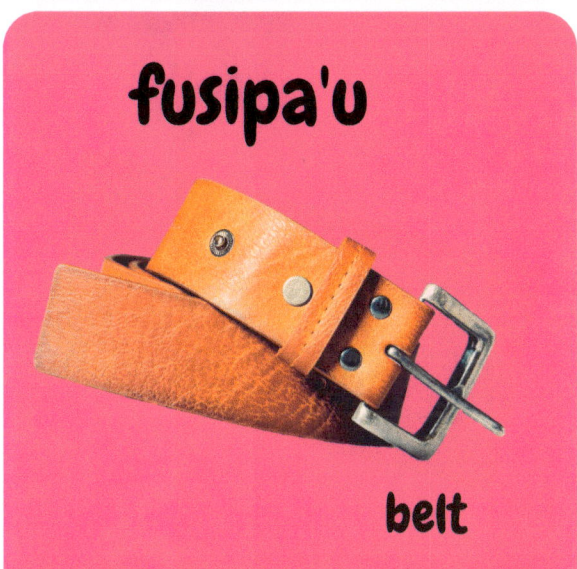

fusipa'u — belt

tusi — book

paluni — balloons

pasika — motorcycle

vine

grapes

fa'ase'e

slide

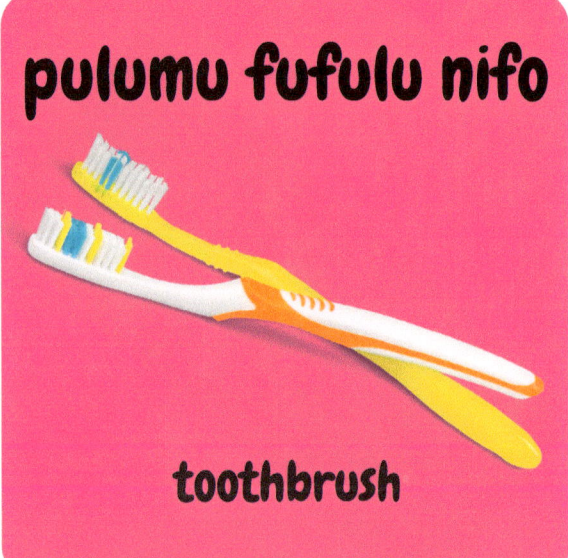

pulumu fufulu nifo

toothbrush

ki TV

remote control

sisi

cheese

pisa

pizza

karoti — carrot

peni vali — crayon

fu'a — flag

fa'amalama — window

kitara — guitar

lake tenisi — tennis racket

tamato tomato	**suō** shovel
nofoa chair	**piano** piano
uati clock	**moli sela** candle

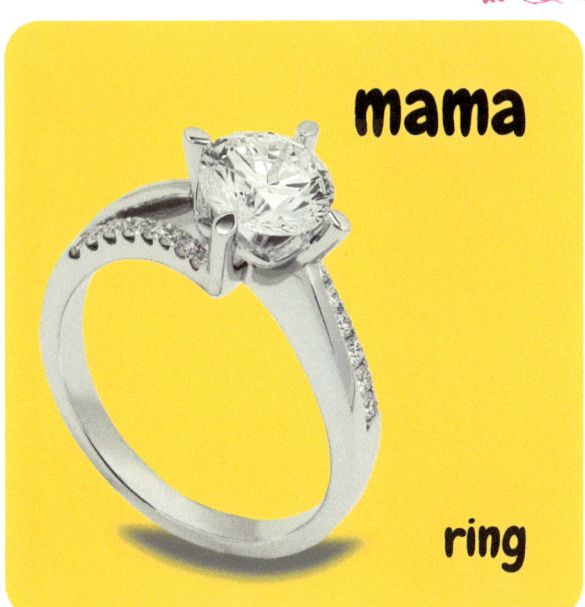

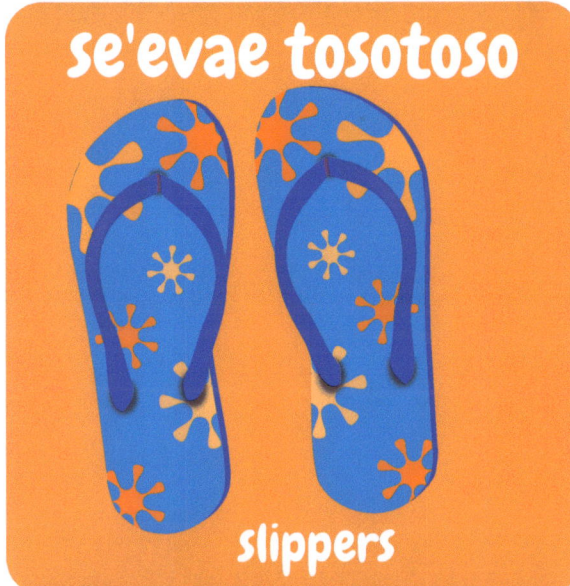

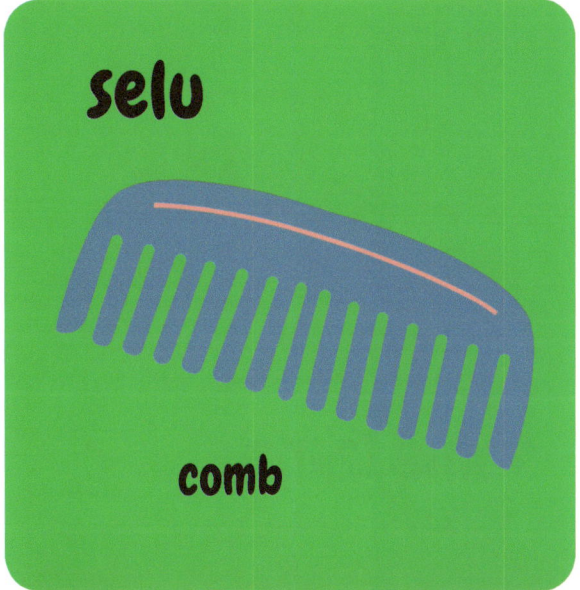

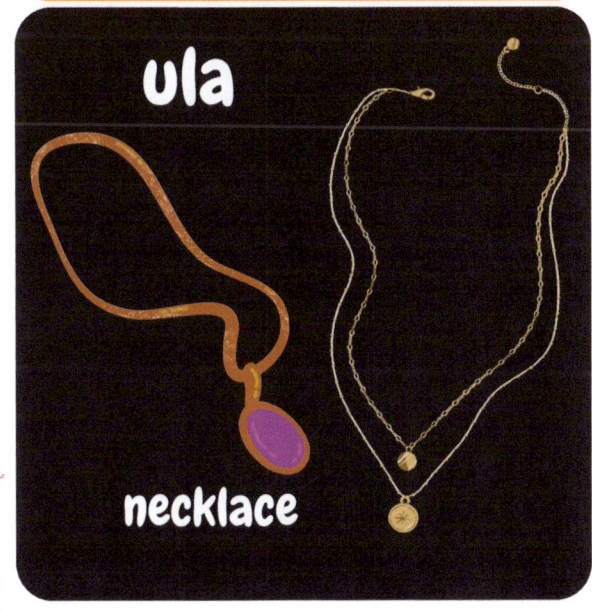

Amoleka here again: Presenting your child's first colours in the final 2 pages. Words in both Samoan and English

mumū
red

samasama
yellow

violē
purple

lanu moana
blue

lanu meamata
green

piniki — pink	**'efu'efu** — gray
'ena'ena — brown	**pa'epa'e** — white
lanu moli — orange	**uliuli** — black

About the Author:

Vaoese Kava "aka" Ese Limutau Noa Aiono has always had a passion for writing since she was a young girl. This later inspired her to complete her Arts and Business Administration studies and earning her MBA from the Australian Institute of Business, South Australia. She's a wife, a mother, and grandmother to the adorable Amulek, Evalyn, and Joseph. Her desire to teach her grandchildren the Samoan language led to the completion of this four-book series of a Child's first 100+ basic words & phrases in Samoan & English. The book series highlights her first grandchild, Amulek Ualesi (Amoleka) and some of his cousins living in different parts of the world.
She hopes that this book series will encourage parents and child to not only learn to read and speak Samoan but practice fun and healthy family lifestyle habits. Follow her on Instagram & Facebook
#VaoeseLimutauKava

I Love You

www.ingramcontent.com/pod-product-compliance
Lightning Source LLC
Chambersburg PA
CBHW041429010526
44107CB00045B/1548